OFF TO THE MOON

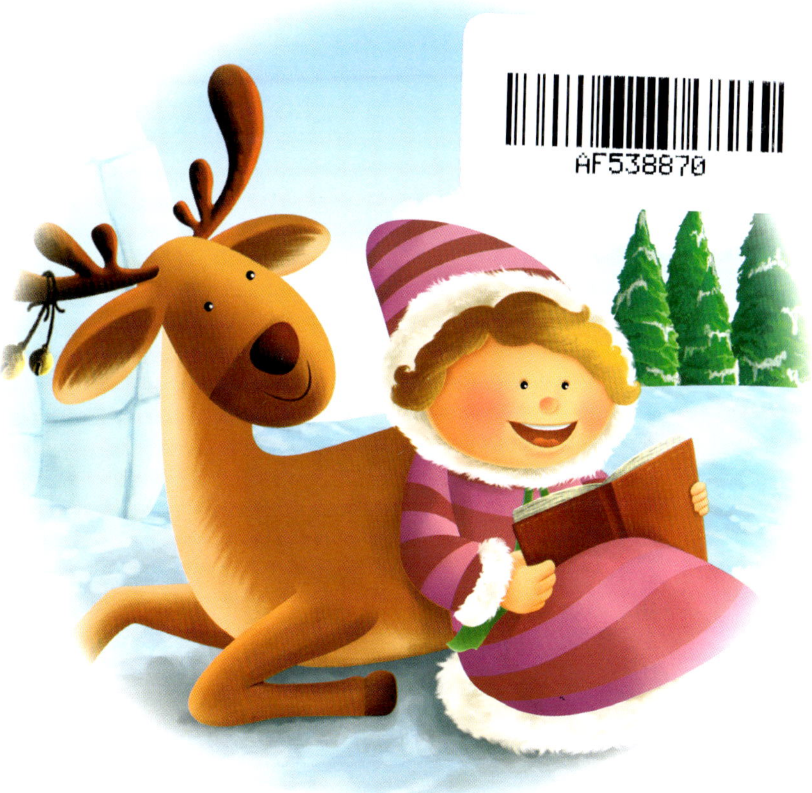

Om KIDZ
An imprint of Om Books International

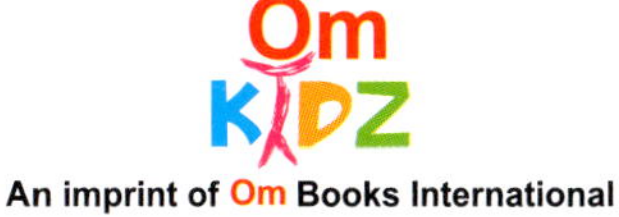

Reprinted in 2025

Corporate & Editorial Office
A-12, Sector 64, Noida 201 301
Uttar Pradesh, India
Phone: +91 120 477 4100
Email: editorial@ombooks.com
Website: www.ombooksinternational.com

Sales Office
107, Ansari Road, Darya Ganj
New Delhi 110 002, India
Phone: +91 11 4000 9000
Email: sales@ombooks.com
Website: www.ombooks.com

ISBN: 978-93-85273-80-3

Printed in India

10 9 8 7 6 5

OFF TO THE MOON

Tiraloo was a little Eskimo girl. She lived all alone in a little **igloo**. **Tiraloo** loved to read books and play with her pet, **Moody** the **moose**.

One day, she read about a man on the **moon**. "How can there be a man on the **moon**?" she wondered. "What is the **proof**?"

Tiraloo did not sit and **brood**. She began to **doodle** on a sheet of paper. When she was done, she happily looked at it. It was a plan to go to the **moon**!

Tiraloo went to her **room**.
She chose her best **boots**.
Then she went to meet **Moody**.

Moody was a very special **moose**. He could fly when he was happy. **Tiraloo** fed **Moody** some **bamboo shoots**. **Moody** loved **bamboo shoots**!

Soon, Moody ate up all the **shoots. Tiraloo** began to read the book about the man on the **moon** to him.

Moody was so happy to hear about a man on the **moon**! His **hooves** were itching to get off the ground. **Tiraloo** quickly put a belt around **Moody** and hopped on his back.

Swoosh! **Moody** flew into the sky! They **zoomed** around the stars and made their way to the **moon**.

Boop! **Boop**! **Boop**! **Boop**! **Moody's hooves** touched down on the **moon**. It was very **cool** and **spooky**.

There was nothing but **moon** rocks everywhere! There was no sign of the man on the **moon**. All of a sudden, they heard a **booming** voice say, "Welcome to my **moon**!"

They saw a short man with a white beard wearing white robes. "I am Mr **Moony**," said the man on the **moon**. "Why did you **choose** to come here?" he asked. **Tiraloo** quickly introduced **Moody** and herself.

Mr **Moony** bowed to them. He looked very **goofy** doing it. "This is how we greet our guests on the **moon**," said Mr **Moony**. He invited **Tiraloo** and **Moody** to his **moon** mansion for dinner.

In the dining **room**, Mr **Moony** asked **Tiraloo** if she would like a **scoop** of **moonberry** ice-cream.

"What are **moonberries**?" asked **Tiraloo**. "**Moonberries** are like **gooseberries**, but they grow on the **moon**," explained Mr **Moony**.

Tiraloo and Mr **Moony** became good friends. **Moody, too,** happily feasted on the **moonberry** ice-cream. **Soon,** they **zoomed** back home. They had lots of stories to tell about the man on the **moon.**

Know your phonic words

These words have the long "oo" sound in them.

Tiraloo	boots	spooky
Moody	bamboo	moonberry
Moony	shoots	gooseberries
igloo	goofy	scoop
moose	choose	swoosh
moon	soon	boop
proof	hooves	booming
brood	zoomed	too
doodle	cool	
room		